# EVERY VOICE COUNTS

## a guide to personal and political action

**By Penney Kome**

**1989**

Canadian Advisory Council on the Status of Women

Conseil consultatif canadien sur la situation de la femme

Prepared for the
Canadian Advisory Council on the Status of Women
Box 1541, Station B
Ottawa, Ontario K1P 5R5

Available free of charge from the
Canadian Advisory Council on the Status of Women
by quoting No. 89-L-156
(The Council reserves the right to limit quantities)



Cette publication existe également en version française sous le titre
*Ce que femme veut... Guide d'action personnelle et politique.*

Kome, Penney

Every voice counts: a guide to personal and political action

Issued also in French under title: Ce que femme veut.
Includes bibliographical references.
"No. 89-L-156"
ISBN 0-662-16720-1
DSS cat. no. LW31-30/1989E

1. Pressure groups – Canada – Handbooks, manuals, etc.
2. Lobbying – Canada – Handbooks, manuals, etc. 3. Women in politics – Handbooks, manuals, etc. 4. Political participation – Canada – Handbooks, manuals, etc. I. Canadian Advisory Council on the Status of Women. II. Title. III. Title: A guide to personal and political action.

JL148.5K65 1989 328'.38'0971 C89-097045-9

# *Table of Contents*

# Introduction

"The country is yours, ladies. Parliament has enfranchised you, but it cannot emancipate you, for that is done by your own processes of thought. Politics is simply a public affair: yours and mine and everyone's . . ."

Nellie McClung, 1917

As we enter the 1990s, Canadian women are demanding meaningful access to power and involvement in decision-making. Women have made some important gains during the 1980s. We lobbied for, and won, legal guarantees of equality in the *Canadian Charter of Rights and Freedoms.* We achieved some success in electoral politics at all levels: federal, provincial/territorial, and municipal. Candidates are routinely called to account for their views on issues targeted by women, and the established political parties claim they are actively seeking qualified women candidates for winnable ridings. The media have begun cultivating women experts as commentators on current affairs. Women have made significant contributions to our understanding of economic change, insisting that our interests be taken into account in the development of policy responses. But, women's work is not done. Most of us still find ourselves confronted by injustice. And many of us, even women who avoid politics, feel the urge to set things right. We want to make a difference, to make our voices count.

Anyone who has ever organized a committee meeting probably has the basic know-how to initiate political action around a hot community issue. Glance through the newspapers – women are doing it all the time. We're organizing around school closings, unsafe drinking water, neighbourhood redevelopment, and any other issue that affects our families and communities. Just as many of our grandmothers were drawn into the suffrage movement through their involvement in social work, temperance, abolition or unionization, many modern women find that the feminist perspective can lend insights into every campaign to regain community control.

Issues often arise so fast that organizers are forced to work by ad hockery – that is, to improvise. This method can be effective (as the 1981 constitutional lobby proved), but it can also mean a lot of wasted effort. Every group should not have to "reinvent the wheel", learning all the basic lessons the hard way.

This book is a guide to personal and political action. It is designed to help you make your voice count. It will help you define your issue and your goals, organize a working group, enlist public support, analyse and work with the media, and take your message to the public and the appropriate authorities. In other words, it will help you bring about change.

# Choosing an Issue

Chapter 1 Checklist

1. Recognize when a personal problem might be a political issue.
2. Redefine the problem as an issue in political terms.
3. Research the issue to bring it into focus.
4. Develop short- and long-term goals for creating change.

## How to choose an issue, or, what to do when an issue chooses you

Most women have so many responsibilities in their daily lives that they do not go out looking for ways to become involved in public issues. Many women hope and expect that their elected representatives will do a reasonably good job of governing. However, some women are extremely disenchanted with the political process and are sceptical as to whether getting involved would make a difference.

Often, women are shocked to discover that the suffragists were right: the political process needs women's participation in order to maintain a realistic perspective. Once drawn into social and political action, women often continue on and work in party politics or run for office. The hard part comes at the beginning: recognizing that something absolutely must be done and that you are the most likely person to do it, then figuring out how to get started. Many veterans say that the first campaign is the most difficult.

The successful 1981 women's lobby to entrench equal rights in Canada's Constitution is often cited as an example of the speed and strength with which women can act. Once women realized what was going on, the overwhelming majority of women's groups and individual women in the general public decided that they personally had to get involved. For many, it was a baptism by fire. The public furor came as a rude awakening to politicians who had accepted weak wording on equality guarantees.

"I was enraged to think we still have to fight for women's rights," a Toronto woman wrote to the Ad Hoc Committee that was the major organizer of the constitutional lobby. "I was coasting along thinking we already were considered equal to men. How foolish of me." Another woman wrote, "I've always considered it was up to the individual to assert her rights, but the (proposed) constitution would take away some of those rights."

Collective action, it seems, is essential to achieving political and social equality. The individual can express her outrage through writing letters to the editor, making phone calls and writing letters to elected representatives, or by calling open-line radio shows. These are all good ways to air a personal opinion. But it's a giant step from individual actions to a collective co-ordinated campaign – the kind that gives public opinion irresistible strength.

Action can be fun. Even when you know that it's mainly symbolic, acting collectively is still more gratifying than fuming privately. Action means getting together with other people to talk things over, finding out that other people share the same concerns, and then taking those concerns to the people in power and publicly demanding that they do something to correct the problem.

## A strong start: How to know when you've found an issue

When you discover that something you thought was a personal problem also affects other people, you may have a political issue. When you hear your friends and people on the street saying, "Somebody ought to do something about this; there ought to be a law", that's an issue.

Feminists have always said that the women's movement goes "from the personal to the political"; that is, from the individual encountering a problem (for instance, not being able to obtain a bank loan without a male co-signer) to the realization that public policy (the banking industry's policy in this case) systematically makes life more difficult for women than for men.

The next step is to ***redefine the problem as an issue***. Personal anguish or outrage has to be set aside for a moment so you can look at how your concern reflects public interest. For instance, several serious instances of toxic waste pollution have been discovered because homemakers have compared notes over the back fence or at the playground and discovered that all of their families were suffering very similar but nameless chronic health disorders. Or they have learned that many pregnant women in the area have either miscarried or delivered infants with birth defects.

As long as the individual woman defines the problem as "My family gets sick all the time", it remains a personal problem. She may try vitamins, exercise, massage, or other home remedies, or make frequent trips to the doctor; however, all these methods may be ineffective in improving her family's health. But when several women get together and redefine the problem as "Suspicion that the local waste dump may be a serious public health hazard", then obviously the problem is a public issue.

## Research can bring the issue into focus

"Research" means gathering facts, placing them in coherent order, and drawing conclusions from them. Research can tell you how many people are affected by the situation you've identified and whether anyone has tried to deal with the problem in the past. It can also help you determine what course of action to pursue. Exhausting as it may be to wade through newspaper clippings at the library, or to go door to door questioning your neighbours, this is a vitally important step in building credibility. **Do not skip it.**

A number of organizations do their own research on women's issues in Canada. If you consult these organizations when beginning your research, you may find that work on your issue has already begun. Government-funded advisory bodies such as the Canadian Advisory Council on the Status of Women, the provincial status of women councils and directorates, and federal government departments such as Status of Women Canada as well as offices like the Women's Program in the federal Secretary of State department or the Women's Bureau at Labour Canada are all good sources of information on women's issues. Non-governmental and volunteer women's organizations are also good sources. For example, the YWCA national office offers an information referral service. Most women's organizations are listed in the directories itemized in the resource guide at the back of this book. Many public libraries either have these directories or can obtain them through interlibrary loans.

While you're at the library, ask the library technician to recommend reference material. Go through the *Canadian Periodical Index* and the *Canadian Newspaper Index*, as well. These useful tools will enable you to scan months of publications in just a few minutes, by looking under relevant index headings.

> ***When the* Charter of Rights and Freedoms *first came up for discussion, Section 15's promise of non-discrimination rights seemed to be a motherhood clause. The government of the day asserted that s. 15 would protect women, minorities, and the disabled from discrimination. Then legal analysts with the Canadian Advisory Council on the Status of Women reviewed women's cases heard under the existing* Bill of Rights *(dating from the Diefenbaker era). They found that the same wording — "equality before the law" — had dismally failed to protect women's equality in several important cases heard before the Supreme Court of Canada between 1960 and 1980. For instance, this wording was interpreted by the Supreme Court of Canada to mean that discrimination on the basis of sex did not occur in sections of the* Indian Act *that denied band membership to Indian women who married non-Indians, or in sections of the* Unemployment Insurance Act *that denied ordinary unemployment benefits to pregnant women. Legal research brought the constitutional debate into focus as an urgent issue.***

## Setting goals

Your final step in defining the issue as political is to propose solutions as well as protest the problem. Before you go public, assemble a list of goals or specific demands within the core group. Having smaller, incremental goals is less daunting and also helps you to measure your progress. You can set one sweeping overall goal and then choose interim goals as steps along the way. Be careful that the objectives you propose cannot be used against you. Make sure your objectives are well thought out and do not create unexpected and serious problems in their implementation.

Always remember, no matter how angry you are, that most of the issues you encounter exist because it's easier for people in power to ignore the problem than to fix it. Much as you may resent bearing the brunt of what is their problem, your job is not to express that resentment, but to put the onus of responsibility back on the people in power.

***Employers often say that women are not promoted because women spend so much time at work worrying about their child-care arrangements that they can't concentrate on the job. In saying this, employers define child care as a personal problem. Women working in corporations, however, redefined the problem as a political issue: lack of employers' support for family life interferes with women's advancement in the work force. Child-care workers redefined the problem from their perspective: lack of public concern for children's welfare both interferes with women's advancement and leaves children at risk for neglect or worse.***

Note how the definition of the problem determines the goals. In this example, research helps bring the issue into focus: employers (and the national economy) are losing valuable productivity from highly-qualified women because child-care arrangements are frequently inadequate. Further, as men become more involved with their children, men are worrying more, and male productivity may be dropping.

For both issue groups, the long-term goal is to provide high-quality, affordable child care for any parent who wants or needs to find paid work. For the child-care workers, the short-term goal is to be able to provide child-care services in good environments with reasonable working conditions. Some may actively lobby for government subsidies for non-profit centres.

Corporate women are more likely to look to their own employers for solutions. For these women, the short-term goal may be to establish a pilot project child-care centre at their workplace. The long-term goal may be to convince employers (using a cost benefit analysis) that, by subsidizing a child-care centre at or near major workplaces, they would gain more in employee productivity than they would pay out in salaries and overhead.

Defining the issue and setting goals are crucial to successful grassroots organizing. Citing research, proposing solutions, and analysing costs and benefits make you credible and better able to persuade others to help you work for change.

# Strength in Numbers



Chapter 2 Checklist

1. Identify your allies.
2. Join others who are already working on the issue.
3. Comb the media to find out what's been reported on the topic.
4. Build a core group of active, committed people, and organize a public meeting.
5. Write yourself a script for meeting people, and use it to enlist others. Rewrite the script as a flyer.
6. Be prepared for opposition.

## Identifying your allies

One essential difference between a personal concern and a political movement is the number of people involved. Once you've decided to take your interest past the letters-to-the-editor stage, you will want to ***identify your allies and increase your support***. Government agencies dealing with the status of women may be tremendously helpful in providing you with research, guidance, and, in some cases, local contacts. Volunteer organizations, community groups, and local social service agencies can help you figure out whether anyone else is already working on what you want to do, or on projects similar enough to be helpful to you.

Dozens if not hundreds of common-interest groups – from service organizations to gardening and literary clubs – are already meeting regularly in most cities and towns. Some of them may have interests that overlap yours. Gardening clubs, for instance, should care about the environment. If your concern is for the environment, attend one of their meetings and see if they're already involved in this issue or are recruitable. ***Join a group*** if you find one working on "your" issue.

Another way to identify allies is to ***comb the media*** looking for references to your area of interest. Start keeping a memo pad and a pencil next to your radio and TV, so you can jot down the names of people who are interviewed and of reporters who cover the topic. In the print media, of course, you can actually clip and keep items pertinent to your project. Again, take note of the reporter's name. When and if your project gets off the ground, you will already have a list of potential allies and of reporters who cover your particular subject.

In all of this preliminary work, you are both educating yourself and looking for the names of people or organizations who may have already done some of the necessary tasks. Suppose you are concerned about the way word processing units are being installed in your workplace. By carefully reading library materials and following stories in the media, you can get the names, titles, and positions of people you need to know, including:

- people at agencies created to carry out research on health hazards on the job, such as the Canadian Centre for Occupational Health and Safety in Hamilton, Ontario;
- union officials and research officers who have done research in order to negotiate for their membership;
- government officials who can explain policies and regulations;
- corporate executives who have participated in management teams studying office automation;
- health professionals (such as optometrists) who treat problems caused by VDT use.

All of these people can be useful to you. Some of them may be so active and productive in "your" issue that you may decide to join their campaign rather than starting your own.

If you have difficulty finding information on your chosen subject, don't be too discouraged. It may just mean that you've become aware of an issue ahead of everybody else. On the other hand, be aware that a total lack of information and total indifference from other people may also mean that you're on the wrong track. To gain public support, it's imperative that you focus on a public policy issue which has affected others. Test yourself: if even the people most affected by the issue start to look glassy-eyed when you present your viewpoint, if even your closest friends try to change the subject or warn you away, then perhaps it's time to find another approach. Be wary of the one-person crusade. It's draining and often futile.

An important issue will usually attract people almost by itself. Spreading accurate information may be enough to build the core group, which needn't be large if the members are dedicated. Five to fifteen committed people can accomplish an amazing amount of work.

***Concerned Farm Women of Ontario started in 1981 with only two women. When they advertised their initial informal meeting, they expected maybe ten women would attend. Fifty-one showed up. Since then, the small (250) but active membership has become financially self-sustaining. They have published two books and produced a videotape. They also have made many presentations to governments.***

## Recruiting people

As mentioned, your community is already organized. If you belong to a group or club, get your concerns placed on the agenda of the next meeting. If you have identified a local group whose interests overlap your issue, try to attend one of their meetings. Identify the main co-ordinator, contact her or him, and find out what activities the group has undertaken. If they have overlooked your particular angle, ask to address the meeting.

If no group already exists, you may be able to ***start a core group*** by enlisting your friends and neighbours. Then there are the time-honoured methods of political organizing: door-to-door canvassing, a telephone lobby campaign (see page 48), notices on community centre bulletin boards, or writing a short article for the community newspaper or workplace newsletter. If you have even two or three people already working with you, consider booking a meeting room, plastering the neighbourhood with flyers, and kicking off your campaign with a public meeting.

## Running a public meeting

Public meetings require advance organization. Unless you're facing a screaming emergency, pick a date at least three weeks to a month in the future. Scout around your area for meeting space: libraries, public schools, and churches often have meeting rooms available at no cost, or for a minimal fee. (You can pass the hat at the meeting to cover your initial costs.) When booking a facility, anticipate the needs of the participants. For example, check to ensure that it is accessible to disabled people and has the necessary power outlets for special equipment. Where necessary, make arrangements for child care, signers (for hearing-impaired persons), and translation. Then design a flyer stating date, time, purpose, place, and any special arrangements you've made for the meeting. If you can persuade a well-known person to speak for your cause, then feature that person's name prominently. You can draw up a flyer by hand or on a typewriter if necessary, but it will look much more impressive if you can get the use of a computer. Many copy shops provide "desktop publishing" (computer typesetting) services for reasonable fees.

While your publicity materials are being prepared, make plans to target them for maximum impact. Select your audience carefully, choosing persons and groups particularly affected by your issue. Then plan your promotional strategy. Many radio and television stations (including cable TV) carry public service announcements (PSAs). Provide them with a short script. Try to "piggy-back" your flyer on another organization's imminent mailout. Supply other organizations with copies of your promotional materials to be handed out at upcoming meetings and take advantage of display literature racks and bulletin boards.

Once you've "got the word out", consider your presentation. You need a meeting co-ordinator at the front of the room to run the meeting and a presenter to express your concerns to the group. As well, it's important to ask someone to record any pertinent points and to get the names and addresses of potential recruits. You may need visual aids. Discussion is often facilitated by having handy a big easel and pad, with a large felt marker for writing down comments as they're made.

Generally, meetings should be planned in three stages: the beginning, middle, and the end. First, the meeting co-ordinator welcomes attendees, outlines the agenda, and introduces the presenter who explains the issue to the group and invites questions or comments from the audience. During the general discussion section of the meeting, the interchange between participants can spark new ideas and initiatives for the group to consider and "bounce off" each other. If the group is large, the co-ordinator should keep track of those who want to speak and call them in turn. This leaves the presenter free to concentrate on answering the questions, encouraging discussion, or writing down suggestions. When the discussion peters out, the group may already have reached consensus on a course of action (which may simply involve forming a committee). If no consensus has been reached, the co-ordinator may suggest a next step. The group approves the action, or calls for further study. The co-ordinator may call for volunteers, whose names and phone numbers should be recorded.

Finally, the co-ordinator thanks the presenter and those attending, sets a date for another meeting (if that's the will of the group), and adjourns the meeting. From start to finish, the whole meeting should take less than two hours. Any longer than that, and people tend to become impatient or lose their concentration.

## Me? Address a meeting?

ait, wait," some of you will be saying. "I have trouble steeling myself to talk to my boss or my child's teacher. How can I go knocking on doors or placing blind phone calls and convincing strangers to join a campaign?" There is a secret to meeting people. Do what the politicians do: ***write yourself a script***. Clarify in your own mind what you want to say. Make your contact brief, courteous, and to the point. Identify yourself, state the nature of your concern, explain why you think the person you've contacted can help you, and ask for something specific.

Rehearse your script out loud until you're comfortable reeling off your message. Get hold of a tape recorder, record yourself, and then play it back, listening to your voice's pitch and inflection. Do you sound squeaky or shrill? Lower your voice and try again. Tense? Smile when you're talking; even when the other person can't see you, the smile can be heard in your voice.

---

**Here's a sample script:**

***Hello, my name is Frances Smith. I live a couple of blocks from here. I'm visiting my neighbours today to find out if you've noticed that your children have had skin, kidney, or respiratory problems while you've lived here, or if you've had problems keeping a pregnancy. My family has had these problems, and it was only when I talked with my neighbours that I realized these concerns seem to be particularly common around here. A group of us are getting together to ask the province to investigate the chemical plant up the road. Would you like to join us?***

---

This script, in various forms, is going to carry you through the campaign. After two days of talking to strangers, you'll find the script rolls off your tongue automatically. You can use your new spiel in personal visits, phone calls, letters, and briefs. The key is to adjust your script to your audience every time. For instance, the neighbourly approach above changes slightly when Frances uses the same script in a call to the Minister of the Environment's office.

---

***Hello, my name is Frances Smith. I'm calling for a group of neighbourhood women who have noticed similar and very serious health problems in our families. I heard the Minister on the radio the other day, and I'd like to know what help your department can offer us in investigating the chemical plant in our area.***

---

Sooner or later, you will want to write your script down on paper so that you can hand it out as a flyer, or deliver it as a brief. ***Writing a flyer*** is like entering one of those contests that asks you to say something in 25 words or less. You want to get a lot of information across in as few words as possible. A snappy headline helps. For instance, from the script above, Frances can write this quick flyer.

---

**Guard Our Children's Health**

***We are a group of longtime neighbourhood residents. We have noticed that our children have suffered a lot of skin diseases and other health problems in the past two years. We are urgently requesting the provincial Ministry of the Environment to investigate whether the local chemical plant is emitting anything that could cause these problems. If you have noticed increased family health problems and/ or if you are interested in working with us, please contact Frances, 555-1212.***

---

To have any credibility, flyers must be signed by a person or group and should give an address, box number, or phone number. For personal security, **avoid** giving any woman's family name and home address on a public flyer. If you must use your home phone number on a flyer, you might be wise to hook up an answering machine as a back-up system. Not only will it take messages from sincere callers when you're out or busy, but you can use it as a defence against obscene callers. Simply hang up as soon as the caller starts using objectionable language, and turn on the answering machine. If the person calls back, let the machine answer. Few obscene callers will risk leaving a recorded message.

## Be prepared for opposition

Sometimes the first sign that an issue is being taken seriously appears in the form of an opposition group. In this case, the chemical plant and perhaps its employees may organize to oppose the community group. Any business, when its practices are challenged, is likely to counter by threatening to close down and remove its jobs and economic support from the community. The community group can respond by offering to work with the business to obtain government clean-up funds; or by buying a company share (if the business is publicly-owned) which allows you to attend a shareholders' meeting where you can raise the issue; or by arguing that human health and lives are more important than any amount of money.

Before you meet or deal with any opposition group or individual, anticipate their response. Within your group, have someone play "devil's advocate" and make objections to your group's position and proposals. Then, prepare your counter-response so that you can force the opposition to deal with your issues, thereby setting the agenda for the discussion. With the opposition on your turf, your chances for success increase.

# Playing their Game?

CHAPTER 3 PLAYING THEIR GAME?

Chapter Three Checklist

1. Big "P" or small "p" politics – two strategy options.
2. Decide whether your group's efforts should be directed inside and/or outside of government.

## Big "P" and small "p" politics

Some women, having done all this preparatory work, will pause at this point and reconsider. Although they feel personally responsible for the well-being of their communities, they're reluctant to use the traditional political route to enter the public arena. They may read a booklet like this one just to see what their options are, but they'll be tempted to find a non-government solution for the immediate problem, if at all possible. Sometimes it seems easier to act independently than to contend with the hassle of the bureaucratic delays, the insensitivity, and the opposition inherent in what some women call "Big P politics". Food banks, emergency shelters, and sexual assault crisis lines all began as non-government responses to the failure of public policy to address real needs.

Ironically, some of the women who are most active and effective in their communities will tell anyone who will listen that they are "not political". They may be involved in schools, churches, synagogues, mosques, libraries; in special interest groups concerned with such issues as poverty and housing; in planning committees; or any of an enormous list of other activities. They may organize countless meetings and bring about real, concrete changes in their communities; but ask them what they think about politics and they'll answer, "Oh, I'm not political at all."

And in a sense, they're right. They're not involved in "Big P" politics, the politics of elections and campaigning and toeing the party line. Dictionaries define "politics" as the art of government; and in Canada, as in other democracies, that means the system of elected representation that has been created to run the country.

Feminists have redefined "politics" as practically anything that has to do with public policy. So, another way to look at "Big P" politics is to place it at the most visible end of a whole spectrum of activities involved in creating public policy. The spectrum ranges from small, grassroots committees working on local problems, through municipal and regional officials (and their support staff), provincial and territorial parties and legislators (and their staff) and, finally, federal officials and the public service bureaucracy. As well, business leaders, lobbyists, and government boards and commissions all have influence at every level.

At the federal and provincial/territorial levels, policy-making might well be called "male" politics. For, even though our foremothers battled to win the vote, the business of government and the party system as we know it are still dominated mainly by men and by male perspectives. Seventy years after suffrage, women are better represented in municipal and regional governments than in federal or provincial/territorial legislatures. Just over 13% of MPs are women (as of the 1988 election). Gigantic barriers continue to prevent women from participating fully in the partisan system – even if they so desired. In fact, many women say that they find party politics hostile and unappealing.

At the same time, women's groups have spearheaded most of the great social changes of this century – changes concerning health, education, culture, religion, the environment, and social welfare. Such groups are actively creating public policy; but usually they don't call it "politics". They call it "getting things done". And they "get things done" outside the partisan structures inherent in legislative office, although they often work with all the political parties active in the relevant level of government.

## Inside or outside?

Frequently, women have worked as outsiders with the express intention of having their goals incorporated into government services. For instance, at one time the only "social assistance" available to most needy families came through women's voluntary benevolent societies. Now, of course, governments at all levels contribute to the support of individuals and families in need.

Some social and political scientists (notably Jill McCalla Vickers and Thelma McCormack) theorize that, in fact, two distinct political cultures operate in most Western democracies. While some women work within the political party system and some men devote themselves to non-partisan organizing, they are the exception, with the result that the style of both forms of social activism can be comfortably described as "male" and "female".

These theorists describe the male system as institutionalized, self-perpetuating, party-oriented, individualistic, and rather rigid. Participants are apt to be motivated as much by personal ambition as by public interest. In contrast, the female system is local, goal-oriented, voluntary, collective, and flexible enough to allow for participants' domestic emergencies. People usually get involved for the sake of solving an immediate problem; when the work is finished, they may drop out or go on to another project.

Parallel to these two definitions of politics, researchers postulate that there are two definitions of power. Governments and political parties seek "power to" – that is, the power and authority to impose their decisions on the electorate. This kind of power is very attractive to ambitious people. Voluntary and lobbying groups seek "power from" – the power and authority generated by true grassroots support. This kind of power tends to be more altruistic or at least well-intentioned.

Women's groups, particularly, find their strength in this second kind of power: the authority of decisions reached by consensus, by recognition of an urgent local need, by support from each other and from the community. Since participants are not competing with one another for personal advancement, they validate and reinforce each other at every meeting and activity. That's why so many women find social activism so gratifying, even though they may not particularly like or share the ideology of other committee members. By coming together in small groups, they receive personal support as well as the satisfaction of achieving important social goals.

The question facing women is whether the comfort and high moral ground of "female" politics is worth the price of being shut out of "male" politics. In recent years, political parties have realized the necessity of finding more women willing to run for elected office. They have understood (quite rightly) that governments could benefit greatly from having women's perspectives represented in legislative debates. And even grassroots women who dislike partisan politics would have to admit that some women MPs and cabinet ministers have been invaluable, articulate advocates for women's rights – despite substantial risk to their own careers in government.

However, there is more than one way to be represented. Women's organizations in this country have built a formidable parallel political structure with the power to force "Big P" politicians to pay attention. This structure is deliberately non-partisan, and many women believe that it serves the public better than whatever government may be in power. Every successful women's campaign strengthens the parallel structure and forces the "Big P" political system to be more attentive and responsive to women's concerns. Moreover, every successful campaign encourages the parties to be more interested in recruiting women candidates.

Distaste for "Big P" politics can be an important factor in deciding how and whether you get involved. You may find the whole system so unappealing that you seriously doubt whether you can grapple with it. Be assured: women have a political potency all their own, quite different from men's. The power and authority generated by women's different political style can be your most valuable asset in tackling male government figures. Women **do not** have to become imitation men in order to be politically effective. If your project has inherent value, you can carry it through without compromising your own values – and, in the process, you might even educate the "Big P" politicians about the importance and value of women's perspective.

# Right on Target



Chapter Four Checklist

1. Figure out under which jurisdiction your issue falls.
2. Start a list of powerful or knowledgeable individuals who have responsibility for your issue.
3. Canvass the people you want to influence and record their opinions.
4. Draw up a scorecard, if only mentally, showing your supporters and your opponents, and what positions they play.
5. Organize a blitz of phone calls, letters, and visits.

Lobbyists should be able to adjust their approach to each situation. A lobbying campaign is like a water hose with a nozzle that can be adjusted from a gentle splash to a strong, stinging spray. The former is good for nurturing friendships, the latter for neutralizing the opposition's resistance. Both tactics are useful, depending upon the situation. And situations do shift. Successful campaigns change all the time, usually because their objective is to change people's minds.

## Who's in charge here, anyway?

Pinning responsibility where it belongs can be more complicated than you'd expect. Jurisdiction is often murky. Hospitals, for instance, are regulated by their own hospital boards, the city or township, and the provincial or territorial health ministry. The provincial or territorial governments, in turn, must meet criteria for funding under the *Canada Health Act*, and purchase-of-service agreements under the *Canada Assistance Plan*. Finally, the federal government provides direct medical treatment in a few special situations, such as the National Defence Medical Centre. A group seeking funds for a new hospital program may be referred from the local level to the federal, and then back to the provincial or territorial, which can use up a lot of time.

Obviously, a fundamental step in developing strategy will be to figure out under which jurisdiction the issue in question falls. Sometimes you will have to present your demands to two or more levels of government at the same time, co-ordinating between federal and provincial/territorial, or provincial/territorial and municipal governments. For instance, a group trying to establish a non-profit women's housing co-operative might seek funding from both the (federal) Canada Mortgage and Housing Corporation and the provincial housing ministry, and also request a zoning variance from the city.

Once again, the telephone is your best tool for sorting things out. Your local community information centre may be able to suggest official contacts as well as volunteer groups. The Blue Pages of the telephone directory will give you general information numbers for most government departments, and the government switchboard operator will try to find somebody in the department who can answer your questions. If appropriate, call your local MP, MPP, MLA or city councillor's office, and ask for the assistance they'd give any constituent.

When calling any level of government, be prepared to place five calls before you find one person who can help. If you get through faster, so much the better; if not, don't take it personally. Persistence pays off in the end. If expense is a concern, call the local constituency office, or contact the federal or provincial/territorial legislature and ask to have the appropriate person call you back.

As a rule, a specific question is most likely to get a specific answer. General questions often fetch very general and fuzzy answers. When doing the initial research before questions are formulated, you may feel you're on a wild goose chase. Don't despair. Keep asking questions and doing your research until you know the specific questions to ask and exactly what information you need. If, after asking these questions, you're not getting adequate responses, call the highest appropriate office: the federal cabinet minister, the provincial premier or cabinet minister, the territorial government leader, or the mayor. Explain your problem and say that you believe you've been getting the runaround. Probably you will get a call back from a senior advisor to the top person, with suggestions and more phone numbers. A referral from the top level can be a big boost in getting co-operation at a lower level.

## Okay then, who's on first?

Even before the jurisdiction question is sorted out, the clever activist will start ***preparing a list of groups or individuals*** who have information and/or power in the area. In fact, two lists would be helpful: one of the people/organizations who seem inclined to help you (allies and ally groups), and one of the people whose minds (and organizations whose positions) you want to change (targets). This latter list includes people/groups who are totally opposed to your cause. Keep track of them in order to outmaneuvre them.

Every smart politician knows that the key to winning elections or to putting a new law on the books is to ***canvass*** the people you want to influence, keeping careful count of who's supporting either side and who's undecided. That's why canvassers go out at election time: as well as recruiting new supporters, they count the votes they expect to get at each poll. They can usually tell in advance which polls they will carry. Smart lobbyists use the same tactics on their opponents, by canvassing the politicians and counting who supports their lobby and who opposes it.

## Keep a scorecard of the players

The names will change, but the scorecard you draw up (if only mentally) for each issue will probably include people in the following positions:

- the minister responsible (or the mayor);
- the minister's (or mayor's) aides and top bureaucratic advisors;
- the opposition critics and their aides and advisors;
- contacts at any government agency or council involved in the issue;
- MPs, members of provincial/territorial legislatures, or city councillors who have been most vocal on the issue, and their aides;
- business people whose commercial interests are involved;
- officers or researchers in labour unions which have taken a stand on the issue;
- media people who are reporting or commenting on the issue.

These are the people on whom the campaign hose will be turned: a gentle flow of information and reinforcement for those who agree with you; a similar gentle flow, with extra cultivation, for those who are undecided; and a strong spray aimed at the opposition in hopes of washing away their resistance. Identifying key players by name means you can direct your efforts where they will do the most good.

***The mayor of a large city and the provincial premier announce a new plan to cut back on the number of people receiving welfare payments. Welfare officers will make random, unannounced visits to recipients' homes, and anyone who isn't home when the social worker arrives will be cut off benefits and have to re-apply. The program will be carried out citywide over a period of three months, and the mayor and premier expect all welfare recipients to stay home until they are visited, or until the program ends.***

In this example, local and national women's groups denounce the plan as an attack on women because the majority of people who rely on welfare cheques are single mothers or elderly women. A women's group immediately calls a public meeting, which draws a huge crowd. The problem and goal are defined as an urgent need to halt what this group calls a sexist and unworkable plan.

Research shows that the jurisdiction is complicated. Welfare funds are provided as follows: 50% from the federal government, 30% from the province, and 20% from the municipality. Although federal influence on the proposal is limited to individual MPs' willingness to twist arms within their own provincial parties, all three levels of government must be lobbied.

In this hypothetical situation, allies are found in the Canadian Advisory Council on the Status of Women and their provincial counterpart; the National Action Committee on the Status of Women (NAC);

the National Association of Women and the Law (NAWL); the YWCA, and practically all the feminist action groups across Canada. NAC and NAWL (through their local member groups) agree to take over lobbying at the federal, provincial, and territorial levels, in close co-ordination with Status of Women activities at city council. Further support can be sought from organizations specializing in this area, such as the National Anti-Poverty Organization (NAPO), the Canadian Council on Social Development (CCSD), and the National Council of Welfare. Other groups which lobby governments on social issues include the National Council of Women, the Fédération des femmes du Québec, the Federated Women's Institutes of Canada, the Junior League, and the Association féminine d'éducation et d'action sociale (AFÉAS).

Targets are identified: federally, the Ministers of Justice, Health and Welfare, and the Status of Women; provincially or territorially, the Minister of Social Services and the Minister for Women's Issues. City councillors find their phones ringing off the hook with irate constituents demanding to know if they support or oppose the welfare scheme. Soon the city's status of women action committee has assembled a list of phone numbers of city councillors who support the mayor's idea. The targets are inundated with a ***blitz*** of mail, phone calls, and visits. Selected reporters begin receiving frequent news releases. They are invited to news conferences featuring representatives from food banks and shelters for the homeless. Within a week, the mayor announces that the plan has been referred to a committee for further study.

# Strategy



From Personal to Political Action Checklist

1. Start with a personal response to the issue.
2. Form a group, and hold a meeting.
3. Draw up action lists: targets, supporters, ally groups, and media.
4. Brainstorm to develop a course of action.
5. Carry out your action, monitor and evaluate its effectiveness, and be ready to persist if necessary.

The Official Channels Checklist

1. Raise the issue during election campaigns.
2. Present a brief.
3. Court the friendly target.
4. Arrange and conduct a friendly meeting.
5. Get the attention and respect of unfriendly targets via telephone, telegram, and letter lobbies.
6. Decide whether to take legal action.

The Public Campaign Checklist

1. Compile a media list.
2. Learn how to write a news release.
3. Learn how to handle a news interview.
4. Designate a media specialist within your group.
5. Hold a news conference.
6. Facilitate coverage for your weekend conferences or demonstrations.

# *From Personal to Political Action*

## Strategy I: The emergency campaign

So far, we've been talking as though a campaign can be planned at leisure. Some issues do seem to go on forever without satisfactory resolution, such as child care, equal pay for work of equal value, reproductive health concerns, and pensions. Other issues, however, appear very quickly and need immediate response. That's when a political novice is likely to be plunged right into action without knowing what to expect.

> ***A flyer suddenly appears pasted on the streetlight outside your home. It says, "Seven women have been sexually assaulted in this neighbourhood within the last month. The police department knows the assailant's methods and general description and has decided not to warn neighbourhood women who are most likely to be the assailant's targets. Women are being used as bait, without even being given a chance to defend themselves. If you are concerned, come to a public meeting at . . ."***

Using this example, here are some ways you can respond.

- **On your own**

Pick up your telephone, call the police chief, and state your outrage at learning that neighbourhood women are at risk. Write a letter restating your opinion and send it to the mayor; send a copy to your local newspaper and to the police chief. Remember: officials find it a lot harder to ignore a piece of paper than a telephone call. Attend the public meeting, sign the petition condemning the police department's methods, and make a donation to the ad hoc group.

• **Forming a group**

At the meeting, you pick up a strategy and information sheet which encourages neighbourhood women to form committees, block by block, to watch each others' homes and to put pressure on City Council and the police department. Also at the meeting, the police department representative suggests that women should treat the issue as a personal problem and offers tips such as, "Don't go out after dark alone", and "Get a man to meet you at the bus stop". Armed with this evidence of unenlightened thinking, you start talking up the issue and soon find eight other women who are willing to form a group.

Start your group's first meeting by choosing a co-ordinator and a minutes-taker, and by drawing up an agenda. Generally, in informal groups, the person who suggests a task ends up doing it. So it's to everyone's advantage to ensure that each member of the group has a chance to speak.

Usually a group gets started by accumulating a list of questions that need to be answered before any decisions can be made. In this case, most of the information has already been presented at the public meeting. In fact, you may be able to use the information sheet as the basis for your script.

Next, have a brainstorming session to assemble the names of people who belong on your ***action lists*** – your group's most valuable organizing tools. At this stage, you're just suggesting names. Later you'll fill in the blanks so that eventually you will have:

- a target list (police chief, police commissioner, mayor, city councillors) with each target's full name, office address and phone number, home phone number (if possible), and full name(s) of the secretaries or assistants assigned to the issue;
- a media list, organized by publication or broadcast station, with names of specific columnists, reporters and/or editors, addresses, phone numbers and extensions, and story deadlines;

- a supporters list, with the names of everyone who told anyone in the group that, "I'd like to help, but I can't come to meetings." Get names, addresses, and phone numbers. They may be willing to write letters or make phone calls.
- a support group list, with phone/contact numbers for the groups' offices or at least two members of the core group or executive. (These will be groups like the YWCA, the local status of women action group, the sexual assault crisis centre, etc.) Also note the frequency of their general meetings, newsletters, and any special resources they can offer, such as office space or skilled volunteers.

Sometimes your list of targets will also include people who might be supporters. Consider this possibility whenever your targets include a high-profile woman who has made pro-woman statements in the past. For instance, suppose your police department recently set up a special sexual assault team headed by a woman and sent her around to give media interviews about the new team. Make her one of your first contacts. If she's already working on the issue, it helps her to be able to say, "I've had 25 phone calls on this already." If she's caught in a conflict and believes she cannot work on this particular issue openly, she'll let you know. She may still be willing to coach you privately, if you promise to be discreet about it.

***Strategy brainstorming*** can be fun. In fact, it can be hilarious. Dream up the most devastating responses you could make, write them all down, and sort through them afterward. Your long-term goal is to change the way the police department investigates sexual assault cases. Your immediate goal is to protect women in your neighbourhood. When brainstorming, think of other short-term goals that would build toward these objectives.

As a representative from the sexual assault crisis centre will probably tell you, there are some traditional ways to protest violence against women. A "Take Back the Night March" for women only (let male supporters babysit and make coffee) can visit and mark the site of each assault. Sometimes groups blanket their neighbourhoods with flyers announcing a "Curfew on Men", or with fake announcements that the area has won an award for having 100% of women graduate from a self-defence course. One neighbourhood committee, facing a similar situation, visited all the local homes and asked residents to leave their porch lights on all night, to improve the lighting generally.

Then there's action on the "Big P" political level, including delegations to the police commission. You can stir up public opinion through forums, workshops, news conferences, picket lines, and demonstrations.

***In Toronto, the Pink Ribbon Committee issued a public request, urging everyone alarmed about violence against women to wear a pink lapel ribbon. Ribbons fluttered from so many lapels and collars that the City Council thought it wise to establish the Metro Action Committee on Violence Against Women and Children (METRAC) to advise it.***

***In Montreal, Action-Travail des femmes mounted a very successful campaign to increase the number of women in municipal blue-collar jobs. First, they informed women when the City would be hiring for nontraditional, nonspecialized, $14.00/hour jobs and organized 150 women to apply for the jobs. When women were not hired, they lobbied the Mayor. When that was not enough, they filled the public gallery during municipal council meetings and dominated the public question period. Women went to the microphones and told city councillors why they wanted the jobs, and why they were qualified. The City of Montreal announced a campaign to hire one woman for every four new positions. This in itself was a major victory. However, women believed they could accomplish more. Action-Travail filed a human rights complaint requesting a 50% quota. On March 7, 1989, the City of Montreal announced that, henceforth, 50% of all nontraditional, nonspecialized, blue-collar jobs would be reserved for women.***

## Strategy II: Chronic local problems

ften, chronic problems have the potential to become emergency situations. To solve chronic difficulties before they worsen, you can apply – in a more leisurely fashion – the same steps outlined above for reacting to emergencies.

***Transportation is often a problem for women, particularly for those living outside urban areas. Women in Whitehorse, the Yukon, faced especially serious obstacles in getting around, both because of the sub-arctic climate and because the city is really a series of loosely-linked subdivisions.***

In this case, Whitehorse women first tried a personal response – organizing carpools – but this system proved inadequate for their needs. Then a group of women banded together, brainstormed, and decided to lobby for a modest public transit system. Because the community is small, they were able to name their probable allies and opponents at the first meeting. Their preliminary market research convinced the township council and the territorial government that there might be enough regular riders to make buses financially feasible. Funds were provided for a pilot project – which the women bid on, won, and operated. After two years, the buses had become so important to the community that they were adopted as a permanent service. To this day, the majority of bus drivers in Whitehorse are women.

For both emergency situations and chronic local problems, your plan of action is basically the same. After careful thought and consideration, react personally, form a group if necessary, draw up action lists, brainstorm to develop strategies and implement your plan. Then monitor and evaluate your progress, and be ready to persist if necessary.

# *The Official Channels*

## Strategy III: Going through official channels

Whatever issue motivated you to reach for this guidebook – whether it be getting a stop sign at your street corner or working towards world disarmament – the usual way to achieve your aim is to influence the people in power. If only you had known in advance how important the issue would be to you, you might have monitored the legislative process for the past several months. As well, you could have worked within the party of your choice to become a candidate – and you might already be in a position where the people in power would co-operate because they know you and owe you favours. But we will assume for now that you are starting from outside the corridors of power and want to get your message inside fast. Sometimes this can be done through official channels: by insistently raising the issue during an election campaign, by presenting a brief to a legislative committee, by lobbying friendly and unfriendly targets, or by litigation.

- **Election time tactics**

On general principle, it is a shame to let an election go by without raising women's issues during the campaign. There's almost always something that needs to be corrected, in any jurisdiction. And this is the time that people who have power or who want power are most accessible. The national Leaders' Debates on Women's Issues during the 1984 and 1988 federal elections proved that, if nothing else, politicians will make an effort to inform themselves on the essentials if they know they're going to be quizzed.

Before every federal election, the Canadian Advisory Council on the Status of Women releases its *Shocking Pink Paper*, a pocket-sized guide on women's issues for voters. It provides you with the basic information you need to quiz the candidates. Between federal elections, the Paper can be used to monitor all parties' actions on their promises.

Look out for election materials produced by non-governmental women's groups as well as by provincial/territorial and municipal status of women organizations. You may even decide to print your own election flyer, highlighting your most pressing issues.

Here are some effective ways to get recognition for your views:

- target one candidate (usually the incumbent) whose track record on the issue(s) has been less than adequate;
- raise the consciousness of all the candidates on the issue(s);
- seek private meetings with candidates;
- arrange an all-candidates' meeting on your issue(s);
- circulate a list of questions (as was done by the CACSW with the *Shocking Pink Paper*), recruit people, and make sure that the questions are raised at every meeting in your ward or riding.

Monitoring party positions as reported in the media will help keep your questions pertinent and up-to-date. Posing a good question means that the candidate cannot wriggle out of it with a generality. For instance, if you ask, "What is your position on child care?", the response can be, "I'm for it." But being **for** something doesn't mean that the candidate will make an effort to achieve it. A more useful question would be something like, "Two months ago, the provincial task force on child care recommended creating a board to license and supervise private-home child care. Do you agree with the task force's recommendations and, if so, what will you do during the next session to ensure their implementation?"

- **Presenting a brief**

All levels of government sometimes create task forces to study issues and to hear submissions (called briefs) from experts and from citizens' groups and individuals before legislation is drafted. These are valuable opportunities to make an impact, so get involved at the very beginning of the process.

The script for your verbal address should provide much of the information you want to present to the committee or task force in your brief: your definition of the issue, facts and statistics (from your research), and proposed solutions. The core group will have to decide which two or three points (at most) you want to stress; any more than that and you risk losing your audience.

You will need to extend your research to get a better idea of your audience. For example, if federal legislation is being planned, contact the Clerk of the House of Commons to get the name of the clerk of the task force or committee studying the issue; and from that person, obtain the names of the people you will be addressing. Library research or personal inquiries will help you identify allies and targets in your audience. Phone an ally or potential ally, and sound her out as to the kind of questions to expect from the members of the task force or committee, and from which members. For instance, one question that usually comes up is, "How much would your suggestion cost?" Prepare your answers: either have figures ready, or else be able to defend the counterargument that ignoring your demands would be much more expensive in the long run.

On the big day, keep your presentation as brief as possible, have it beautifully typed, and bring some extra copies (in both official languages, if necessary) for distribution to committee members and/or the media. Your delegation should be punctual and look professional. Choose your spokesperson for her ease in addressing groups. If you need technical expertise, bring along a resource person to answer tricky questions. Circulate a news release before the meeting, announcing the key points you'll be presenting, and then hold a news conference afterwards, to talk about how you were received.

As an alternative to presenting a brief, you may be able to wrangle an invitation to address a legislative committee considering a draft bill that has already been presented to the government. However, this is more likely to be a formality. Once a bill has been introduced, major changes are unlikely – short of a massive public uproar. Still, making a good impression on the committee can be a solid foundation for any possible subsequent action.

## Strategy IV: Lobbying friendly and unfriendly targets

Between elections and task forces, you'll have to find other ways to get your message to your targets. Start with the friendly approach: send a letter or a brief and then follow up a week later with a phone call asking for a response and/or an appointment. Be polite, but be persistent. Remind your target (or assistant) of the ways he/she will benefit by being sensitive to your concerns. Be nice until you have to be not-so-nice. But always be professional and persistent. Often being nice will suffice. If you can't get immediate agreement, get an appointment.

- **Arranging meetings: Your place or mine?**

Usually, a person in power will expect your group to come to his or her office for an appointment. This arrangement has several advantages for you: all the relevant files and papers should be handy; other people in the office can be consulted; a small meeting can be very direct and to the point.

Occasionally, perhaps at election time, you may prefer to have the target come to meet your group. This strategy has the following advantages: you may feel more comfortable on home territory; you may be able to show the target some specific instances of the problem you're protesting or the solution you're proposing; you can invite your supporters and ally groups to the event; a larger meeting gives more people in the group a chance to participate; and a promise made before a larger group is harder to disavow than a promise made to only two or three people.

Whatever the venue, you will want to make the most of this opportunity. Re-write your script, pitching it to your target's interests and jurisdiction. Provide a written copy for your target's file.

When organizing a public meeting, long-standing women's lobby groups have found the team approach helpful. The person who is most comfortable speaking in public does the introductions and most of the talking, while the person who is most familiar with the subject matter provides the back-up. It's a good idea to bring someone to record the meeting on tape (get permission first) and/or to take notes. You may also want to bring a fourth person to observe body language, aides' reactions, and other valuable clues. Teamwork gives moral support and lets each of you concentrate on her own job.

Your target's job, meanwhile, is to make you happy without adding to his or her workload, or making promises that are difficult to keep. Therefore your target may treat you to reminiscences of childhood, philosophizing about the role of government, or complaints about how other women's groups have behaved. When your target starts rambling, you should politely pull the conversation back to the topic you want to discuss. You might say, "That's very interesting", and return to the issue at hand.

By the way, if the friendly (or unfriendly) target has done anything with which your group wholeheartedly agrees, then you should certainly say so at the beginning of the meeting. People in public life hear an awful lot of complaints. A little bit of honest praise might just win you a staunch ally or soften an opponent's resistance.

- **The unfriendly target**

Targets sometimes do not return their phone calls, or call back only to convey bad news. Sometimes people in power need to be convinced that your presentation expresses widely felt public opinion and not just that of a few non-conformists. And sometimes a target's own beliefs prevail, regardless of public opinion. When a target refuses to be won over, then it's time to show that you can make a fuss that cannot be ignored. You want to show that your blessing can make someone popular, and your anger can make their lives miserable. Here are some time-honoured methods of lobbying politicians and corporations by having your supporters make personal contact.

***Telephone lobbies*** are an excellent way to multiply the impact of a small group. Pull out your list of supporters and support groups, count them up, and decide what you want to ask them to do. Call each person on your list, ask her to take part in the lobby, and then ask her to call five more people and persuade them to do the same. Theoretically, starting with five people, on the fifth go-round such a tree would reach more than 15,000 people. Of course, all those people will co-operate with you only if they agree that the issue is urgent and important. So you'd better have a good motive and write yourself a good sales pitch. Make it easy for others to help you: give them the information they need (phone number, address) and advise them to ask for something specific (a meeting, project funding, a supporting vote).

Telephone lobbies can be activated quickly as a sledgehammer response to, say, a politician's offensive remark. It can disrupt a person's whole day when dozens of indignant people tie up the office telephone lines demanding an explanation – but it can also give the person a chance to explain or to reconsider.

***Telegram lobbies*** can be put into action almost as fast as phone lobbies and offer a speedy, inexpensive, and convenient way to send a message to another city or town. Telegrams still have a certain political mystique that enhances their effectiveness, and can be sent to several people simultaneously. With just one phone call apiece, thirty-seven people, each sending telegrams to eight MPs, could blanket the House of Commons quickly. CN/CP Telecommunications (look in your Yellow Pages under telecommunications) offers a special low rate for Public Opinion Message telegrams of 15 words or less, addressed to members of Parliament.

***Letter lobbies*** take some time to organize but are well worth it for ongoing issues. Usually your target will feel obliged to respond to each personal letter, if only by setting up a form letter on the office computer. Your core group should draft a sample letter, then copy and distribute it to lobby participants. For the most effective response, urge them to write their own personal letters rather than mail in the form letter. Remind the people helping you that no postage is required for letters addressed to a member of Parliament, mailed within Canada. Letter lobbies also give you a chance to explain why you think the issue is so important. A good, short (one page) convincing letter can sometimes get you an interview even when your phone calls aren't returned.

How do you know whether your lobby has been effective? Sad to say, you might find out the bad news from the newspaper. But good news, when it comes, often arrives as an invitation to come in and talk about your issue.

## Strategy V: Legal action

Sections 15 and 28 of the *Charter of Rights and Freedoms*, which were won with such effort, have provided women in Canada with powerful new tools for combating discrimination based on sex, race, religion, and other prohibited grounds. Some experts believe that these tools are not being used often or effectively enough. The determination of women's groups to use them whenever possible could advance the cause of equality immeasurably.

> **Section 15:**
> (1) *Every individual is equal before and under the law and has the right to the equal protection and equal benefit of the law without discrimination and, in particular, without discrimination based on race, national or ethnic origin, colour, religion, sex, age or mental or physical disability.*
> (2) *Subsection (1) does not preclude any law, program or activity that has as its object the amelioration of conditions of disadvantaged individuals or groups including those that are disadvantaged because of race, national or ethnic origin, colour, religion, sex, age or mental or physical disability.*
>
> **Section 28:**
> *Notwithstanding anything in this Charter, the rights and freedoms referred to in it are guaranteed equally to male and female persons.*

The *Charter of Rights and Freedoms* has proved to be a two-edged sword. When women strategize and work together for a common cause, the Charter can be used to cut cleanly through discrimination. But others have also wielded the Charter to their own advantage. For instance, one court struck down a Criminal Code provision against a man having sex with an underage girl, because there was no similar penalty for a woman having sex with an underage boy.

Moreover, constitutions change. Just as women were beginning to explore the potential of the equality guarantees in the Charter, the federal and provincial governments agreed to amend the Constitution in many important areas. Some organizations, including the Canadian Advisory Council on the Status of Women, believe that the wording of the Meech Lake Accord potentially affects the Charter and women's equality guarantees.

Last, but far from least, Section 33 of the Charter permits federal and provincial governments to "override" or opt out of Charter provisions for a maximum of ten years. Section 33 can be used to suspend Charter rights won through litigation. For instance, people who are opposed to freedom of choice in reproduction have lobbied the government to invoke s. 33 and pass legislation contradicting the Supreme Court's decision on abortion.

***Section 33:***

*(1) Parliament or the legislature of a province may expressly declare in an Act of Parliament or of the legislature, as the case may be, that the Act or a provision thereof shall operate notwithstanding a provision included in section 2 or sections 7 to 15 of this Charter.*

The other four subsections in s. 33 specify that a law passed under the override clause shall have force for a maximum of five years, with a five-year re-enactment allowed. Note that s. 33 does not apply to s. 28, the clause that women's groups helped to word, and fought desperately (and successfully) to exempt from s. 33. However, s. 33 does apply to the sections on which most of the equality cases (so far) have been based.

You may find redress through the courts if the issue that concerns you is a dispute with government, any government agency or service, or an employer or landlord. After doing your research, consider seeing a lawyer if you believe that what you are facing is a violation of equality rights. Some YWCAs run legal clinics, with no charge for the initial consultation. Or, if you live near a university with a law school, there may be a free legal clinic or a local chapter of the National Association of Women and the Law (NAWL). The Women's Legal and Education Action Fund (LEAF) may be able to refer you to a lawyer in your area. Even if you never actually proceed to litigation, threat of court action can be a big inducement to get the other side to sit down with you and talk reasonably. You will still need to research your issue and build an activist group of supporters.

Consider the potential for legal action when faced with a case that appears to constitute sex discrimination by any level of government, government agency, or government-regulated or government-funded enterprise. LEAF suggests using this question as a guideline: "If this case went to court, would the results have an impact on other women?" You may never actually go to court, but presentation of a well-prepared legal challenge has proven to be extremely persuasive when dealing with recalcitrant governments.

***The International Coalition to End Domestics' Exploitation (Intercede) is an organization representing domestic workers, most of whom are immigrants and almost all of whom are women. For years, Intercede tried to persuade the Ontario government to provide labour code protection for domestic workers. With LEAF's help, Intercede prepared a solid legal challenge (based on the Charter) asserting that domestics were not protected because they are women. The province responded with legislation to the effect that domestics who are asked to work more than 44 hours a week must be given compensatory overtime pay or time off in subsequent weeks.***

# *The Public Campaign*

## Strategy VI: Media relations

Sometimes the easiest way to get your target's attention is to make your issue sound so important that he or she seeks you out. Most politicians have aides who comb the news media daily, looking for issues that will make them look bad – or good. If you choose to go the public route, **always remember: you cannot control the media**, once they get hold of a story.

Stories gain tremendous credibility by appearing in the news media. Perhaps you have noticed, on things you know about, that sometimes reports agree with what you know, and sometimes they don't. Usually, the difference is the reporter covering the story. If you don't already pay attention to bylines, now is the time to start. Most newspaper and magazine articles carry the writer's name at the beginning, right under the headline or title. Broadcast reporters "sign off" with their names.

If you have been collecting clippings, sort through them now to see if any particular reporters' names come up consistently. Those names are the beginning of your ***media contact list***. As you notice interested TV and radio reporters, jot their names down too. When you contact ally groups, ask them if there are any reporters, editors, or columnists they especially cultivate.

Before long, you'll have a working list of people who are likely to take the time to read your news releases. Whether the item gets ink or airtime depends on deadlines and other news breaking that day. Luck and timing are vitally important. Your news may be eclipsed or enhanced by simultaneous events.

- **The news release**

News releases can be used to notify the media of an upcoming event, to recap the highlights of a meeting or speech, to respond to current events, or any other time that you want to get a statement into newsrooms quickly. Groups, rather than individuals, usually issue news releases and the group is always described in the last paragraph. **Always include a name and phone number for the media to contact if they want to follow up on the story – and be sure to respond as quickly as possible to their calls.**

Try to choose one reporter or editor in each newsroom and address the release to that person by name. Send extra copies of the release to pertinent columnists and editorial writers. Some groups still assign members to race around the city delivering news releases by hand. If at all possible, it's much faster, easier, and more impressive to send releases by FAX machine. It is not unusual to follow up a news release with a phone call, a day or two later, to clarify any points on which the reporter has questions.

It is important to remember that newsrooms usually receive dozens of news releases every day. Check the calendar for upcoming events that might bump you off the news lineup. However, even with the best of planning, there's an element of luck in getting news coverage. If a bigger news event comes up, your release may be ignored, despite its importance.

Don't send out a news release if your story isn't newsworthy; you don't want to be a victim of the "cry wolf" scenario and be dismissed by assignment editors. However, even if your issue isn't a hot topic, you may want to send a feature release which may be used as resource material by feature writers.

Be imaginative in preparing your release. Package your message attractively (for example, have it printed on paper of a different colour or shape). However, don't be too cute; if you're doing something out of the ordinary, do it in a way that is appropriate and relates to the content of your release. Practice and experience will help improve your "batting average" in getting your message across to the media.

Writing a news release is similar to writing a news story, except that you send it out on letterhead. You want to get all five W's (Who, What, When, Where, and Why) as close to the beginning of the story as possible. Here is a sample news release, showing the formula:

**[date]**

OTTAWA [**Where**] – The Canadian Advisory Council on the Status of Women (CACSW) [**Who**] released today [**When**] an historical examination of women's participation in all levels of Canadian politics. *Women in Politics: Becoming Full Partners in the Political Process* is a background paper [**What**], designed to stimulate greater participation by women in the governing of our country, our provinces/territories, and our municipalities [**Why**].

"The key to women's full equality in all areas of society," said CACSW president Sylvia Gold, "will be our increased participation in the political process." [**Quotations are important in a news release; always use two or three.**] According to the CACSW paper, women's access to politics is impeded by such factors as a lack of financial support, the attitudes of political parties toward women, the difficulty of juggling a political career with family responsibilities, and the lack of support services such as adequate child care.

"The 1984 federal election saw a dramatic breakthrough in the number of women elected," Sylvia Gold said. "However, the gains are modest from an historical perspective." Although the proportion of women elected has increased from 0.4 percent in 1968 to 9.9 percent in 1984, the paper estimates that, at the present rate, it will take decades before women enjoy equal representation in the federal Parliament.

The CACSW, established in 1973 in response to a recommendation from the Royal Commission on the Status of Women, is an independent organization funded by the federal government. The Council's mandate is to bring before the government and the public matters of interest and concern to women in Canada. [**Bottom paragraph always identifies and describes the group**.]

For more information, contact [**name and position**], at (000) 000-0000. [**Always give a contact phone number, and fax number where applicable, and be sure someone's there to answer the phone.**]

- **The news interview**

Media response to a really interesting and provocative news release will usually be a request for an interview. If you agree to be interviewed, it goes without saying that you should be thoroughly prepared to discuss the issue intelligently. Have plenty of facts, figures, and anecdotes at your fingertips. It's a good idea to have ready three key messages or points you want to make. If you've never been interviewed before, you might want to rehearse, with a friend playing interviewer.

Reporters ask a lot of questions that may sound obvious to you. Sometimes that means the reporter is checking your answers against other information. Sometimes the reporter needs to have basic information explained in your own words in order to produce an interesting story. And sometimes the reporter knows absolutely nothing about the issue and needs to be briefed from the ground up. Your job is to be informative and remain courteous. If necessary, cite sources for background information that the reporter can look up later.

Always assume that everything you say during an interview will be quoted publicly. That's the whole purpose of the exercise. "Off the record" comments are risky; some news outlets have a policy against honouring such requests. If you don't want a comment attributed to you, you can, of course, politely decline to answer questions, refer the reporter to someone else, or offer to get back to the reporter when you've had time to double-check your facts. Do not guess at information or try to mislead the reporter. If the reporter is asking an obvious question as a way of checking your replies against other information, you just lose credibility.

Be wary of such questions as, "In contrast to your position, another women's group has made such-and-such a comment on this issue. How do you respond to that?" The question is designed to stir up conflict, because conflict is news. Unless you know from other sources what the other group said, and your group has decided on a response, you're probably wise to duck the question. Say, "I wasn't aware they had made that comment, and I'd like to talk to them about it before I respond publicly." Also, be careful about agreeing with a question like, "That other group is really weird on this one, eh?" If you say yes, you may find the words attributed to you. Smile and say, "I'm not prepared to comment on that."

Ideally, one member of your core group should begin to specialize in media relations. Your ***media specialist*** should be free of other responsibilities during public events so that she's always available to help reporters. Between events, she should be easily accessible by telephone.

- **The news conference**

Reporters prefer exclusive interviews, but they will attend a news conference when it's the only way to get important information. Usually the people giving the news conference read a prepared statement, distribute copies, and then field questions. Coffee and snacks may encourage reporters to stay. For best results, try to schedule news conferences – and distribute news releases – early in the week, and before noon. That way you're likely to slide in under everybody's deadlines.

- **The weekend conference or demonstration**

Getting coverage for a weekend conference or demonstration requires careful planning and advance publicity. Look more to the broadcast media than to print. Broadcasters have to work weekends anyway. You'd be amazed at how much of your Saturday or Sunday newspaper is typeset the previous Tuesday.

Although the news release announcing the conference or demonstration will probably stress the size of the event and the qualifications of participants, reporters who attend will most likely be looking for colour and detail. You can help them by providing:

- thumbnail biographies of the speakers;
- copies of the speeches;
- detailed programs describing the workshops;
- an informed person constantly available to help arrange interviews, locate organizers, and give directions;
- a quiet media room for private interviews;
- typewriters, telephones, and extension cords;
- coffee, juice, and snacks.

By the way, media-bashing is a popular but rarely productive pastime among groups. It's a serious mistake to start "bashing" the reporters who respond to your news releases or cover your events. After all, they took the trouble to come out and listen to you – maybe even had to argue strenuously to get the assignment. Although media relations may seem like an adversarial process at times, there's no sense looking for a quarrel with a journalist. The journalist will always have the last word – and publicly.

# Eternal Vigilance

CHAPTER

6

ETERNAL VIGILANCE

Collective action has brought women in Canada closer to full equality than the suffragists ever could have dreamed. Where women were once warned that it was against nature to expect equal pay for doing the same work as men, now women have the confidence to demand equal pay for work of equal value. Still, eternal vigilance is required, not only to advance towards total equality, but to protect the advances already won.

Perhaps the most important lesson to be learned from our limited experience with the *Canadian Charter of Rights and Freedoms* is that non-discrimination rights are only as strong as the women's groups which defend them. Constant vigilance is required to protect equality rights. Every organized women's lobby and every well-prepared legal argument serves to educate the public, even (as occasionally happens) when it doesn't reach its other objectives.

The methods outlined in this guidebook are designed to apply to a wide assortment of situations, because women tend to be pulled into social and political action for a variety of reasons. Hopefully, once you have acquired the skills necessary for organizing social and political action, you will want to remain active. "Big P" politics and politicians affect every aspect of your daily life. Ultimately, only you can decide – through watchfulness and immediate action when necessary – whether the impact of your efforts will be helpful.

Just before the House of Commons voted on whether to include Section 28 in the Charter, every member of Parliament received a personal invitation that read, in part:

> "WE INVITE YOU to strengthen further the Charter with respect to women's equality . . . You can be assured that we will be continuing our work for constitutional improvements on behalf of the women of this country. AND WE INVITE YOU to support us in these efforts."

The invitation remains open, both to elected officials and to members of the public. Whatever you may think of politics or of governments, whether you choose to work from within the system or from outside it, your voice counts and your participation is vital to making Canada a better place in which to live.

# Resource Guide

# *Government Contacts*

## Federal

The following women's groups exist either within the federal government or are independent, though funded by the federal government.

The **Canadian Advisory Council on the Status of Women** is an independent organization funded by the federal government. The Council's mandate is to bring before the government and the public matters of interest and concern to women. Its extensive research on women's issues is published as books, background papers, and fact sheets, copies of which are available free of charge.

Canadian Advisory Council on the Status of Women
110 O'Connor Street
P.O. Box 1541, Station "B"
Ottawa, Ontario K1P 5R5
Distribution Centre (613) 992-4976

**Status of Women Canada** advises the Minister Responsible for the Status of Women, co-ordinates policy analysis of issues affecting women on inter-departmental, federal-provincial and international levels, and communicates government priorities to women's groups, non-governmental organizations, and the general public. Their publications include a *Directory of Federal Government Programs and Services for Women*. All publications are available free of charge.

Status of Women Canada
151 Sparks Street, 10th Floor
Ottawa, Ontario K1A 1C3
(613) 995-3901

The **Secretary of State's Women's Program** provides financial and technical assistance to women's organizations and other voluntary groups for activities that promote the equality of women in Canadian society.

Secretary of State
Women's Program
25 Eddy Street, 11th Floor
Hull, Quebec K1A 0M5
(819) 994-3202

Another **Secretary of State** program, the **Aboriginal Women's Program**, administers grants exclusively for Aboriginal women's organizations and provides Aboriginal women's groups and individuals with resource information. The program is administered through Secretary of State regional offices. For a list of their locations, write to the national office below.

Secretary of State
Native Citizens Directorate
Aboriginal Women's Program
Ottawa, Ontario K1A 0M5
(819) 994-2135

The **Secretary of State's Disabled Persons, Participation Programme** offers important services to the disabled persons' community, including grants for non-profit disabled persons' organizations and free publications on issues of interest to disabled persons. They also publish a *Directory of Resources for Disabled Persons.*

Secretary of State
Disabled Persons, Participation Programme
25 Eddy Street
Hull, Quebec K1A 0M5
(819) 997-2412 or 997-2413

**Women's Bureau, Labour Canada** consults with other government divisions and non-governmental groups on issues of concern to women in the labour force. It also conducts and publishes research on these issues and provides information for interested groups and individuals through its extensive reference centre and its free publications. The Women's Bureau administers a small grants program designed to assist projects and events related to women's employment issues. The Reference Centre is open to the public and handles requests for the Bureau's free publications.

Labour Canada
Women's Bureau
Ottawa, Ontario K1A 0J2
(819) 997-1553

**Sources**, a directory listed further on in this guide, is an excellent tool for contacting members of the federal government.

### All levels of government

The Blue Pages section of your local telephone directory is a good source of general information. You can use them to find the main numbers for government departments and agencies, including federal and provincial Human Rights Commissions.

The offices of your local MP, members of the provincial/territorial legislature, and city councillor/regional representative can help you track down contacts and/or information within their respective levels of government.

## *Non-governmental Women's Groups*

Many non-governmental women's organizations are excellent sources of information, research, and contacts. The directories listed below contain extensive listings of these groups, as well as many governmental women's organizations. Most public libraries either carry these directories or can order them for you through interlibrary loan; or you may wish to purchase a personal copy from the publishers.

## Directories

The **Canadian Women's Directory** lists advisory councils, feminist publishers and periodicals, and national organizations, as well as women's groups by subject within their respective provinces. (Bilingual)

**Canadian Women's Directory**
Les Éditions Communiqu'Elles
3585 St. Urbain Street
Montreal, Quebec H2X 2N6
(514) 844-1761

The **Index to Canadian Women's Groups and Directories** lists women's groups and organizations, databanks, as well as directories and related publications, nationally and by province. (Bilingual)

**Index to Canadian Women's Groups and Directories**
Office of the Portrayal of Women in Programming
Canadian Broadcasting Corporation
P.O. Box 8478
Ottawa, Ontario K1G 3J5
(613) 738-6579

The **Directory of Associations in Canada** provides an extensive list of women's associations in the subject index under "women". (Bilingual)

**Directory of Associations in Canada**
Micromedia Limited
158 Pearl Street
Toronto, Ontario M5H 1L3
(416) 593-5211
(800) 387-2689

The **Sources** directory lists many women's organizations, within and outside government, both alphabetically and by subject. It also has a special section listing federal government contacts, including a guide for contacting members of Parliament and the portfolios of cabinet ministers, and opposition critics.

**Sources**
The Directory of Contacts for Editors, Reporters and Researchers
9 St. Nicholas Street, Suite 402
Toronto, Ontario M4Y 1W5
(416) 964-7799

## Databank, Lists, and Labels

The **Canadian Women's Movement Archives** has produced a computerized list of all women's groups in Canada. **Fem-Direct** allows you to access women's groups by province, city, postal code, and by area of interest or concern. The IBM-compatible computer disks come with an easy-to-follow user's manual. You can also order printouts of lists and labels from the databank.

**The Canadian Women's Movement Archives**
P.O. Box 128, Station "P"
Toronto, Ontario M5S 2S7
(416) 597-8865